May 2, 1974

To Lillimae Hester

in deep appreciation

Newport, Harbor

Costa Mesa

Board of Realtors

*Dedicated to the people of the United States
by the Realtors® of America.*

Contents

Under all is the Land

Under all is the land. Upon its wise utilization and widely allocated ownership depend the survival and growth of free institutions and of our civilization. The Realtor is the instrumentality through which the land resource of the nation reaches its highest use and through which land ownership attains its widest distribution. He is a creator of homes, a builder of cities, a developer of industries and productive farms.

Such functions impose obligations beyond those of ordinary commerce. They impose grave social responsibility and a patriotic duty to which the Realtor should dedicate himself, and for which he should be diligent in preparing himself. The Realtor, therefore, is zealous to maintain and improve the standards of his calling and shares with his fellow-Realtors a common responsibility for its integrity and honor.

In the interpretation of his obligations, he can take no safer guide than that which has been handed down through twenty centuries, embodied in the Golden Rule:

"Whatsoever ye would that men should do to you, do ye even so to them".

Published by National Association of Real Estate Boards, Chicago, Illinois

One Land

During the formation of the earth when time was not measured by the minute, nor the booming sound of a Westminster chime or on the page of a scenic calendar, a mass of rock was thrust up through a raging sea. There were no human ears to pick up the sounds nor were there eyes to witness this movement. It was that moment in time when the birth pangs of a land of the future began: the land to be known as the United States of America.

Winds and rain hurled themselves against this rocky cornerstone, and in the process of time the waters gave way and more rock, steaming in the hot sun, joined with the first.

A miracle was taking place, but before the quiet and peaceful scenes we know today could be realized, more tortures, more cataclysms and more upheavals would be required. Fire and ice, earthquakes and floods bent and buckled the original rocks, changing forever the shape of this new-born land.

Time passed, and life appeared on the land.

Since primitive man first daubed pictures on the walls of caves, painters, poets, writers, orators and more recently, photographers have all sought to capture in their particular disciplines the impression left on their minds by the land. So varied is this huge land that there is little or no duplication of impressions. Each eye can see it accurately, each brush stroke can reflect its imagery with acuteness. But words are, at best, poor substitutes for actual experience, and thus the writer and orator find difficulty in expression, for in all this majesty of land, air and sea the restrictions of the language become most apparent.

Creation determined inevitably the position of great land forms: the snow-capped Sierra Nevada, barren Death Valley, the rich Mississippi deltaland and the beautiful eastern seaboard. It gave man the mines of Kentucky, Utah and California, the wide open range lands of Texas and the Midwest, the orchards and groves of California and Florida, and the forests of the Paul Bunyan country.

From the highest point, 20,320 foot Mount McKinley to the lowest, Bad Water set at 282 feet below sea level in Death Valley, from the icy, wind swept Diomedes in the Bering Sea to the balmy beaches of Florida and Hawaii, there is a common link called unity, a link between man and nature whose offspring is the United States. Creation gave to man a grave responsibility. He was to use that land for his own well-being, but he was also to protect and nurture it for generations yet to come. How well he has succeeded in doing this is the story of the United States. It evolves around a word which today is the nation's conscience: conservation.

For the most part the story is a happy one, but there are dark sides to it which, mercifully, are being overcome. Never before has man been so vitally aware of pollution problems, land utilization and the flagrant waste of resources. This awareness is good, for one need only read Steinbeck's *The Grapes of Wrath* to see how good land, rich land, can be turned into a bowl of dust. Ahead still lie many problems such as water and air pollution, but man and his land are coming to a closer understanding.

The rivers of America, from the broad Mississippi to the bubbling trout streams, are the life lines of the nation. Without them the land would be stagnant. Imagine the country without "Ole Miss", the Ohio, the Hudson, the Columbia, the Platte or the Colorado. If even one were missing the land would be hard pressed, for each river has its own individual purpose which none other can replace.

Sometimes these rivers seem lonely as they flow silently and murkily to the sea from which all life sprang. But as they edge their way across the land they carry tiny particles of soil which grain by grain build up into a rich deltaland, which in turn produces crops of foodstuffs for man.

Old Man River never sleeps he just keeps rollin' along and as he rolls he turns hydro-electric generators which keep the homes and industries of the nation humming. But in the mountains, where many great waterways have their humble origins, the rivers fulfill a different purpose. Here, water means life for the countless number of tiny fingerlings that wriggle in the gravels of sparkling streams before starting out on a survival race to the sea—often, according to the cycle of their specie, only to return to spawn and die at their place of birth.

Men have gone into the mountains following the river highways to seek precious metals in the rocks or dig for gold in the gravel bars. They have used the rivers to float logs to screaming sawmills and the huge pulp and paper mills which are so vital to the economy of the land.

Here, too, high up in the mountains this man-creature can escape from his humdrum city life and commune with the land,

perhaps with rod and fly, canoe and hiking boots, camera or gun.

In some places the mountains dip down into the sea to provide unforgettable vistas of fjords, ice and tall green timbers. Here the land becomes awesome as it stands in solid defiance against the onslaught of a powerful sea. But there are also regions where surf gently rolls onto sandy shores and beauty takes on other forms.

Man has named the seas that wash his shores the Pacific, the Atlantic and the Caribbean. Just as the names are different, so is the land they serve. The sharply indented Atlantic seaboard provides hundreds of harbors of refuge and commerce, while the more easily defined western coastline has restrictions placed upon it by nature.

For as many people who gain their livelihood from the coastal regions of the land, as many meet the land under vastly different circumstances. No sea breezes blow across the central plains. The winds blow hot and cold and man thinks not within the confines of a city block, but in square miles and open spaces.

The land, ever changing but changeless, has been the driving force of the nation. As such, it has molded men and women to give each a slightly different outlook and appreciation of his particular allotment of *terra firma*. It teaches him, it influences his way of life, sustains him, worries him. But it must be obeyed, for in this vast space of mountains, prairies, lakes and streams there is nothing more insignificant than man.

The glorious color of the Garden of the Gods, Colorado.

11

wind-swept,
urled tree
Dome
untain,
semite.

The struggle
for life in
rainless
Death Valley.

13

The blinding White Sands of New Mexico.

The counterpane of the Midwe

A flower of the desert.

Under all is the land, and it is a good land, but it must be loved and utilized to be appreciated. The original pioneers were farmers and they loved this land because it was their own. The great American statesman and educator Daniel Webster once said, "When tillage begins, other arts follow. The farmers, therefore are the founders of human civilization."

The spread of the land across widely different climatic zones means the farmers can grow a variety of crops, such as fields of golden grain, sugar cane or luscious oranges and other fruits and vegetables. It also provides cotton from which clothes are made, forest lands, sand pits and mines for building materials, and it lines the pockets of the "founders of human civilization" with dollars.

Oranges; the golden lamps of Florida and California.

16

The land of the kings of the sport of kings, Kentucky's Bluegrass country.

Crop dusting the cotton fields of Texas' Rio Grande Valley.

17

For all its richness, though, the land must be nurtured. In some parts of the country life-giving water seems to be everywhere, but in the dry-belt areas it is as precious as the richest treasure and must be brought in by irrigation and the parched land, by a miracle, becomes fruitful.

If the land governs our way of life, so does the sea which washes its shores and the rivers which drain it, providing sport as well as food.

Home on the range in Utah.

Mechanized cotton picking.

Old fashioned cat fishin' and modern St. Louis.

Irrigation, the life ditch of Te

Tobacco, a premier crop of the American South.

Following the seagulls over the deep green sea.

San Francisco's Fisherman's Wharf.

A kingfisher surveys his world.

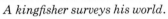

Buffalo survey their home.

*America's
highest waterfall
in Yosemite
National Park.*

*High living
Big Horn sheep
rule the land
they survey.*

20

Peaceful setting in New England.

Shrimp boats, Mississippi delta.

In Florida's Everglade

Oregon Coast.

An inland lighthouse near Plymouth.

Utah's Great Salt Lake.

Torch lighting ceremony in Hawaii.

Burning sugar cane, a step on the way to America's sweet tooth.

From the barren tundra of Alaska to the lush jungles of Hawaii; from the orange groves of California and Florida to the patchwork plains of the midwest and the gentleness of New England, we have seen the land in its many forms. Like the young lady amid the flowers of Hawaii millions of Americans have found peace and contentment in the land, for all are part of it, even those who dwell in the concrete jungles of the city.

ing shadows fall on the scrub vegetation and the surf
ds the beach at Maui, one of the Hawaiian Islands.

Many Cities

Man is a creature of order. Throughout his turbulent history, always there has been a seeking to create order out of chaos. And often the first influence Man attempts to control is his immediate environment.

This need to control his environment stemmed from man's well-defined social order. He was concerned about the safety and comfort of his family. He sought ways to improve their way of life. Finally through trial and error he developed his first rude shelter of leaves, sticks and mud.

From that moment on he hasn't stopped building.

Huts became houses, groups of houses became towns and the more prosperous towns became cities. An innate sense of line and form developed over the years and different styles of architecture appeared. In the passage of time these styles became known by various names, such as Romanesque, Gothic or Colonial. The highly developed sense of social order, which was a prime factor in the survival of the race, inevitably led to the concept of town planning.

These ideas, with few exceptions, came relatively late to the land which was to be known as the United States of America, but when men and women from the Old World ventured to the New, they made up for lost time with a vengeance. Pioneer towns along the Atlantic seaboard grew into cities and as the land was opened up new cities were spawned, pushing westward to the shores of the Pacific Ocean. Embryo cities sprang up everywhere. But only the strongest and fittest of these could survive, for in those glorious days of destiny when a continent was being opened up, rugged free enterprise, competition and sheer hard-headedness—and sometimes the Colt revolver—were the rulers.

The early cities and towns were not gracious; that glossiness came later, and when it did come, it put a stamp of character on the city. New Orleans, for instance, grew up intrinsically different from New York, San Francisco from Los Angeles, and so on. Different types of industries helped mould these communities; geography too played its role, and of course, the temperament and origins of the people put the polish on the man-made creation.

So then, if every city is different, what is a city?

Everyone has their own concept of a city, but is it easy to find a true definition? Is size the criterion? New York, with a population of 8.5 million, is one of the world's largest cities, a city which seems to embody everything that is great about this country; but metropolitan Reno, with a population of only 120,000 also claims to be a city of world status, "the biggest little city in the world". Then there are the innumerable little hamlets scattered throughout the land which boastfully call themselves cities. Obviously a city cannot be defined purely in terms of size. Perhaps the difficulty lies in the name.

Substitute the antiseptically clean words "urban environment" and you lose the spirit of the city—that's it! The spirit of the city. This is the defining quality, for the spirit can be found in big city and small hamlet, thus the two enter the arena hand-in-hand; only the scale of measurement differs and the term "city" becomes applicable everywhere. A city then is a place where the spirit of man dwells, a place he calls home, a place where his roots are established, where he works and plays. And it is the place which he defends with all his might against those who have the temerity to say that another place is better than his.

Opposite page 27, we see a girl buying an ice cream cone from a street vendor. The locale is New York, but the spirit leads girls all over this great nation to munch on ice cream cones, so there is really nothing uniquely New York about this picture: but on the other hand, an operating oil well in the Capitol building grounds could only represent the spirit of Oklahoma City.

The spirit of the city manifests itself in a variety of small ways. One common "spirit" of all cities seems to be the pigeon. The universal, strutting, pompous but lovable pigeon. They are to be found nesting in the eaves of stately public buildings, taking over parks and town squares and almost demanding to be continually fed from sun-up to sun-down.

Strange too how continual roadwork seems to be a common denominator of all cities. Travel to any number of cities—particularly in the summertime—and you'll find the work crews digging up the sidewalk or the pavement, and the traffic policemen wearing that look of hopeless frustration on their faces, as they deal with a problem which every day grows greater and more unsolvable.

These are some of the little poignant spirits that infiltrate the avenues and boulevards of our "urban developments".

But the most important spirit is that of industry, for it dictates in no uncertain terms what form urbanity will take. The great steel industry has forged out cities like Pittsburgh, whose products, in turn, have created other industrial complexes such as Detroit. And those are only two examples of a chain reaction which has created such a healthy economic climate that no force on earth can stop, match or beat.

The spirit of industry, however, wasn't strong enough to do all this alone. It needed a companion spirit, so it drew on the inquisitive spirit of man. This combined force led man to found schools—from little red brick schoolhouses to great educational palaces, such as Harvard, Yale and the Massachusetts Institute of Technology.

There is a drawback, however, to the spirit of industry. It is faceless, while the opposite gives man his greatness. Many people say that cities are faceless too, but that is to be unfair, for the city has a mood and this mood is reflected on the face of the people, who are the spirit of the city. Walk down any street, stand at the corner and watch the passing parades. You will see happy faces, worried faces and lonely faces—the universal triumvirate of all cities.

And these people you are watching seem always to be in a hurry. Is this because they are caught up in a measurement that man created when he set about to put all things in order? Is it time, measured by the hands on a wrist watch or on the town hall tower? The answer is partly yes. Clocks have to be punched, alarm clocks ring, trains and buses go on time, maybe there's time for a quick cup of coffee before a timed appointment, clocks on parking meters have to be fed on time, and then there's lunchtime, sometimes tea-time and suppertime, time for a favorite TV show and finally bedtime. Fortunately, it is not just for these reasons the crowds rush by.

Time is important to the young and brash, and the United States is both young and brash. Its cities are growing so fast, its productivity is increasing so rapidly, its technology is so ever changing that there is no time to let the grass grow underfoot.

Even buildings which, a generation or two ago, were considered the architectural marvels of their day, or homes whose style was once the height of fashion, fall victim to time and the wreckers' hands. In their place arise gleaming buildings of steel, glass and concrete, beautiful but functional, in which armies of people mill about seeking the will o' wisp of fame and fortune. Sometimes these changes in the appearance of the city are called "redevelopments" and in many instances they are good, but to the sentimental the passing away of familiar landmarks is a sorrowful occasion, as part of the spirit that they knew so well is extinguished. But before long a new skyline fills the void and the spirits rise again as the old gives way to the new.

Nature knows only two times: daytime and night-time. Man and his world—his time—must adjust to the natural laws. And so when daylight changes into darkness the cities, the towns, the country and the people change as well. The drabbest of skylines during daytime hours can suddenly be transformed into a brilliant fairyland of sparkling color. A solitary light burning in a farmhouse on the Midwest horizon has a beauty like a solitaire diamond flashing on the finger of a young lady. The brilliant lights of a high rise apartment or a skyscraper office building sparkle like a tiara

at first night at the opera, and the glow of factory lights and flames add richness to the exciting panorama.

The spirit of beauty was with man in his prehistoric cave. On the gloomy, sweaty walls of his primitive home he crudely painted familiar scenes and as his skills developed, so did his taste for line and color. All these things have progressed with him through the milleniums of his building addiction.

No other nation on earth has cities with such tall shafts as can be found in New York or Chicago, nor the luxury that is evident in the hotels, motels, homes and apartments that dot the land. Even the humble Alaskan fishing village has a chance to break into the big time as the result of oil discoveries in a state whose wealth has hardly been touched. A small town in the Midwest might have just the right natural resource close at hand to attract new industry. The day of the instant city is at hand.

It may well be that the future of the Alaskan community or the Midwest town is already being planned in the silence of

an office building in that most American of all cities, New York.

Stepping inside one of these air-conditioned, sound-proofed office buildings is like plunging into the cool, peaceful depths of an ocean valley while a storm is raging overhead.

Nowhere in Nature is there a parallel to man's ability to produce so much noise—both in quantity and variety. And the city seems to act much the same as a magnet—attracting soundwaves that bounce from building to building and oscillate from one deafening crescendo to another.

But not all is lost however, for fortunately man also learned the finer art of producing sound of a pleasing nature. For every harsh discord there is a compensating harmony.

Stand in any city and listen. You will hear the strains of great symphonies and operas from splendid auditoriums greeting the night almost hand-in-hand with the rhythmic beat of exotic drums and blaring brass from some tiny, smoke-filled bistro. Move on and you will hear the hushed sounds of hidden conversation in a dimly-lit restaurant or cocktail lounge. Or perhaps it will be the muffled roar of traffic from the canyons downtown or the tail-end of a political argument or a juke-box bellowing away at a discotheque. Perhaps it will be the slamming of a door, a jet streaking overhead or a cat and dog fight in an alley.

Many sounds, many people, many spirits—and many cities.

New York is the business center of the nation, and the western world. As Wall Street dictates, so goes the country. Side by side with financial leadership, it sets the pace for fashions, the theater and other fields of the arts. Its towering spires to God and Mammon awe the viewer as no other skyline in the world does, even though it has many rivals.

On the other side of the continent, San Francisco demands
attention and puts up lively competition to New York. But
the greatest attribute of this City by the Golden Gate, and
the feature that sets it apart from all other cities, is its
magnificent natural setting and spacious harbor. Like its
eastern rival, it is a cultural center too, with such offspring
as an opera company and symphony orchestra which have
gained international repute.

Founder William Penn called Philadelphia "a greene country towne" back in 1681, but you couldn't call it a "country towne" now. Today it is a major transportation and industrial center, ranking third in the U.S. hierarchy of giants. Known far and wide as the "city of brotherly love" it has within a 30-mile radius more buildings and historic memorabilia connected with the American revolution than any other city.

33

Boosters of Chicago will say "so what" to the claims of others to the role of leadership. They point to the fact that Chicago leads everybody in the production of steel, machinery, cosmetics and even snuff. And there is another side to Chicago whose impact on the United States—and the world—is difficult to assess, for many far-reaching decisions are made at the numerous conventions which meet here. Chicago, the nation's second largest city, has a per capita income higher than the nation's average and is home to the world's leading agricultural markets.

34

For many years, 130 in fact, Pittsburgh had the reputation of being
the "Smoky City" due to the steel mills and coal mines which give
this "gateway to the west" city its very being. The war on grime has
been successful, however, and because of its achievements in the realm
of urban redevelopment, Pittsburgh has earned for itself the title
"City of Progress". The cost has been in the billions of dollars, but this
expenditure has proved that pollution and redevelopment—two of the
nation's greatest problems today—can be solved if bold and
imaginative steps are taken.

35

Miami Beach

The junior "big city" of the
United States is Miami. Warm
waters and winters give Miami that
"something" which the industrial
giants of this country cannot hope
to have. Businessmen, as well as
tourists, are finding their way to the
tip of the Florida peninsula and
discovering that Miami is the
panacea for all the tensions and
pressures of the business world.

The charm of New England.

Sailboats against the Boston skyline.   *Harvard, America's first university.*

The pounding surf of the Atlantic seaboard.

A New England motel (<u>nee</u> wayside inn).

New England, the first section of the United States to be finished and achieve stability.

In a city there must be a sanctuary, a niche where the body and mind can relax. The green grass of a park, the shade of a tree, a monument or piece of sculpture; these are things most city dwellers seek.

Fortunately people are not all alike, otherwise the spots mentioned above would be so crowded there wouldn't be places to relax. So we have people who get their pleasures in other ways. It might be by preaching the Gospel on a street corner, or by becoming a hippie.

The universal sanctuary is, of course, the home. It might only be a tarpaper shack or a luxurious apartment in a high rise prestige block; it makes no difference.

'Mid pleasures and palaces
though we may roam,
Be it ever so humble,
there's no place like Home.

When an American goes through the door of his home he leaves all the work-day cares behind and enters another world, that of his family. Here lies the strength of America.

Louisville, Ky.

New York

Chicago

Chicago

Los Angeles.

San Francisco

Calico: gone but not forgotten.

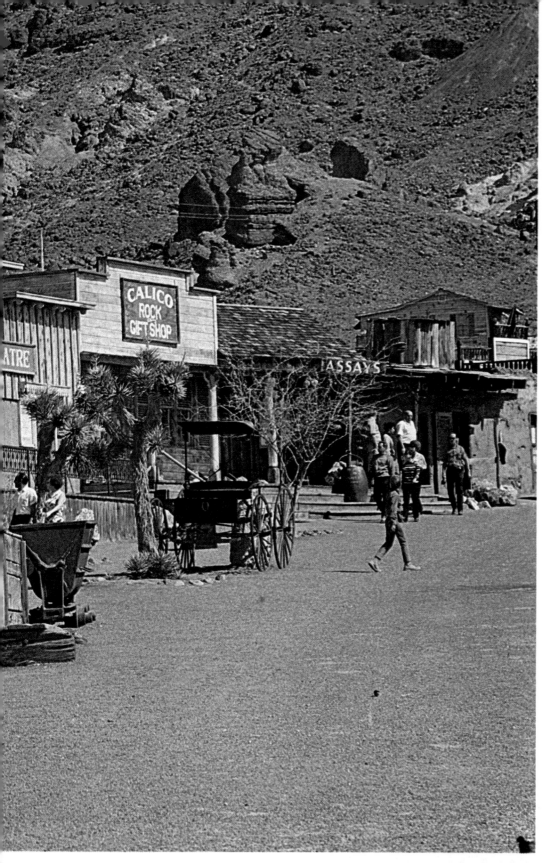

There is a certain eeriness in the sight of a town that has been by-passed by progress, but it is no use lamenting for those who put their faith, their money and their effort into its founding. In the lustiness of life in the United States everything from a Banshee jet to a town is expendable if something better comes along.

And so today the West is dotted with the gaunt remains of once-proud buildings and towns. These "Ghost Town Gothic" buildings which echo to the sound of creaking doors and snapping shutters are a romantic lure to adventure.

To some, a place that is now a ghost town was once a home, a place which was loved, sometimes a place of sorrow, but above all, a place of memories.

Calico, California, and Virginia City, Nevada, share a common heritage and in their ghostly appearance they leave a message. The miners thought they had the best, but the best is always yet to come. Perhaps with new mining techniques, these old camps will suddenly emerge in the Space Age as bustling cities once more, as indeed some already have. But to those whom progress has passed by, they survive as reminders of an exciting era when life in America was in the raw.

For Sale.

43

Society Hill, Philadelphia.

Boston Common.

Music Center, Los Angeles.

Cities are always on the move, and
most of the time the people are, too.
There are occasions, however, when it's
good to sit down and let the world go by.
A ride on a San Francisco cable car
can be relaxing and so can another
popular pastime, feeding the pigeons.

Temples to God and Mammon.

San Diego's Spanish influence.

The pagodas of Los Angeles.   *Gaslamps in Old Charleston.*   *New Orleans' French Quarter.*

Alaskan church.

Fishing village in Alaska.

The Old Worlds of East and West mingle quite freely in American cities.

A farm in Vermont.

49

San Francisco, the Fireman's monument.

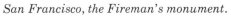

Denver, Capital of the nation's highest state.

San Antonio, a bit of Venice in Old Texas.

Chicago, a vestige of yesteryear.

Salt Lake City, an oasis in the desert.

Oklahoma City, cattle and oil.

San Francisco, the old East and modern West.

Sun-bathed Waikiki.

Anchorage, the key to Alaska.

Chicago!

No two cities in the United States are identical and none can be truly compared with another. Each has its own distinctive appearance and its own mood. These are often keyed to its heritage—that of man or of nature.

Move San Francisco's Chinatown to Las Vegas and it would seem incongruous; transplant Oklahoma's oil wells to Waikiki and the people of Honolulu would be happy, but the effect would spoil the particular beauty of this Hawaiian scene.

Las Vegas in daylight.

Miami; gracious living from the air.

New York! The city that has everything. New York, the nation's largest city.

It is said that 49 million Frenchmen can't be wrong about their country, so it is that 8.5 million New Yorkers cannot be wrong about their city. In this great city of tall buildings, crowded streets and great cultural and financial institutions beats the pulse of the nation. It is the mecca which attracts many an aspiring tycoon, actor or artist; it is the city which challenges the world and accepts this challenge without fear or favor.

For millions of Americans, the Statue of Liberty, which greeted them as they steamed up the Hudson River, was a beacon of hope for a better life in a new world. Here in New York millions of immigrants were absorbed into the American main stream, sometimes bewildered by the fast pace and the vitality of its life. But no matter from what part of the world a person may come, New York will make him feel at home.

In such a cosmopolitan city, therefore, it seems natural that the "capital of the world" should house the headquarters of the United Nations. In this imposing glass-faced building, in front of which fly the flags of member nations, many far-reaching decisions are made to preserve peace and order in the world. While part of New York, in actual fact it neither belongs to the city nor to the United States; it belongs to the world.

Like the United Nations, New York is the place where everybody gets together.

This Heritage

My country,
'tis of thee,
Sweet land of liberty,
Of thee I sing:

In the simple words of a great national hymn, Americans pay fond tribute to a rich, colorful and varied heritage which in no little way is founded on the words "democracy" and "liberty".

Every flagstaff in the land carries visible proof of this heritage—Old Glory. A symbol that speaks proudly of a nation whose heritage has spread to the four corners of the world.

One of the glories of this heritage is that it is infused with that of other nations, a skillful blend of the best from the best. But in the final analysis, what emerges from this brew is something essentially American.

A heritage is an evolutionary process; it has no date for a beginning nor does it have an ending. The American heritage started long before the European set foot on this land, for whether the white man recognizes it or not, the native Indians have a heritage of which they are justifiably proud. And they were here a long time before palefaces became civilized in their lands.

From a calendar point of view, the date September 8, 1565 could well be said to be the moment when the cornerstone of the United States was laid. On that day, "with many banners spread, to the sound of trumpets and salutes of artillery", the Spanish under the command of Pedro Menéndez de Avilés founded St. Augustine, Florida—America's oldest city. This was 42 years before the Englishman, Captain John Smith, founded Jamestown, Virginia, and 55 years before the *Mayflower* (shown in replica on the opposite page) arrived off what is now Plymouth, Mass. For 200 years Spain held St. Augustine. It then came under English rule, and in 1821 was taken over by the United States. Ralph Waldo Emerson called St. Augustine the "little city of the deep", and although there are no structural remains of this "first", the heritage is preserved and continued in the family name "Solana" which appears in a marriage register dated July 4, 1594. During the short-lived English regime, colonists from Minorca were brought to the area. Two descendents of these people were Stephen Vincent and William Rose Benét, who added richly to the heritage of American letters.

Spain planted the first colony and introduced Christianity to what is now the United States, but England brought the beginnings of a democratic system. On May

13, 1607 Captain John Smith launched England's second attempt to colonize North America. The first, under Sir Walter Raleigh at Roanoke, Virginia, ended in disaster. Smith's romance with the Indian maiden Pocahontas has enriched the American heritage, but Jamestown means·more than that to the American way of life. It was here, in 1619 that the first representative government, elected by popular vote, established the principle of self-government. On November 20 of the following year another landmark was reached aboard the *Mayflower* when 41 adult male Pilgrim Fathers signed a Compact "to combine ourselves together into a civil body politic, for our bettering order and preservation . . . and by virtue hereof enact constitute and frame such just and equal laws, ordinances, acts, constitution and offices, from time to time, as shall be thought most meet and convenient for the general good of the Colony; unto which we promise all due submission and obedience."

Conditions in the Thirteen Colonies were ideally suited for the furtherance of democratic thinking. Vast distances separated them from the authority of London, and within a quarter of a century following the Pilgrim Fathers' landfall, England was ravaged by civil war. The challenge of unlimited open spaces also sparked thoughts of liberty in the minds of the colonists.

Idyllic thoughts, however, were interrupted by the ever present danger of Indian attack, and many a bloody page was written into the annals of early America. But marauding Indians were not the only source of anxiety. To the north the French were expanding their influence, and in the south La Salle had taken over the lower Mississippi region for France, calling it Louisiana and establishing a post in Texas. By 1709 there was war between the French and the English, and this would continue until 1759 when the sun finally set for France on North America. Engaged in these bitter battles was a Virginia planter by the name of George Washington. At that time, Thomas Jefferson was growing up in the Blue Ridge country of Virginia.

Following the defeat of France, England rather clumsily tightened up its colonial administration, creating much resentment

Faneuil Hall, Boston, "Cradle of American Liberty." Here fiery patriots urged action against England.

in the Thirteen Colonies. Some blundering pieces of legislation were enacted and stirrings of revolution were heard. In 1765, nine colonies, led by New York and Massachusetts met in New York to debate the Stamp Act, which required revenue stamps to help defray the cost of keeping royal troops in the colonies. This meeting adopted a Declaration of Rights which opposed "taxation without representation". Virginia added her voice to the growing dissension when Patrick Henry warned London of the consequences if the laws were enforced, stating: "If this be treason make the most of it!" The laws were repealed in 1770, except for the one levying a tax on tea, but time was running out. On March 5, 1770, English troops fired on a mob in Boston and three years later a cargo of tea was thrown overboard from a ship in Boston harbor. As a result, the port was closed, town meetings and elective representation were suppressed until the money was raised to pay for the tea. To secure the rights of the colonists, the First Continental Congress met in Philadelphia from September 5 to October 26, 1774. England, however, wouldn't budge from her decision on the status of the colonists and the voice of Patrick Henry was heard once more, this time before a revolutionary convention in Richmond, Virginia: "Give me liberty or give me death!"

On the night of April 18, Paul Revere began his famous ride to warn Lexington of the approach of English soldiers, and in the words of Henry Wadsworth Longfellow, "The fate of a nation was riding that night." The next day the Minutemen went into action, and the collapse of royal rule in the colonies began. For the colonists there could be no turning back, and the great victory at Bunker Hill spurred them on. On June 13, George Washington was named commander-in-chief and a system of government deriving its authority from the people began to take form. It was this driving force "from the people" that led to the momentous meeting in Philadelphia on July 4, 1776. At this meeting a document written by Thomas Jefferson was presented. It was called the Declaration of Independence.

The impact of Jefferson's words "that all men are created equal, that they are endowed by their Creator with certain unalienable Rights, that among these are Life, Liberty and the pursuit of Happiness" spread to other lands, particularly to France and oppressed Poland. The Marquis de LaFayette and Tadeusz Kosciuszko joined the ranks of the first of the world's "freedom fighters" and when the war was finally over they took the American ideals back home with them.

The hue of the New England maple leaves changed six times before the noise of battle ended with the surrender of Cornwallis at Yorktown on October 19, 1781. Monuments of stone now dot the once-bloodied fields of Concord, Lexington, Bunker Hill, Long Island, Bennington,

France's gift to the U.S., the Statue of Liberty.

Saratoga, Valley Forge, Bemis Heights, Vincennes and Yorktown, and all those who treasure the heritage of the United States remember and are grateful to those who suffered and triumphed in the name of Liberty.

The war over, there now began a heritage of achievement. In 1803 the United States acquired Louisiana, and the next year Lewis and Clark set out to make the first American overland crossing of the continent. Three years later Robert Fulton made the first practical steamboat trip aboard the *Clermont*, and in California, where Spain ruled, the missionary work begun by Father Junipero Serra in 1769 was being patiently carried on by his successors.

In the background, though, war clouds were extending from the wild frontier where unfriendly Indian bands prowled to "the shores of Tripoli". Relations between the United States and Britain were also strained, and this led to one of the most senseless wars in history. The war of 1812. All the issues at stake had been settled, but word did not reach North America until after hostilities had broken out, and in the two years of carnage that followed, both the United States and Canada felt the trod of invading armies. The White House and the Capitol Building were burned. Some historians say it "began in nothing and ended in nothing", but that is not quite true for something did evolve from the ordeal. First came the words of the National Anthem, and closely behind that, a sense of national unity which turned the eyes of the country to the Great West.

It was the era of the frontiersman, of men like Kentucky's Daniel Boone who, in his old age sought the open prairies west of the Mississippi. And Davey Crockett, who temporarily foresook the outdoor life in 1821 to go into politics, winning a seat in the Tennessee legislature—largely, it is reported, by his ability to tell stories. Crockett, in death, became immortalized. In 1835, Texas, led by Sam Houston and Stephen Austin, proclaimed its independence from Mexico and a provisional government was formed. Mexico, however, did not give up its claims easily. In San Antonio, 180 brave men held out for liberty for 13 days in an old mission building called the Alamo. They all died; among them Davey Crockett. A month later, on April 21, 1836, with the cry "Remember the Alamo!" on their lips, the Texans defeated their enemy at San Jacinto. Nine years later the Lone Star state was admitted to the Union.

Adventurous Americans, as far back as 1841, had been crossing the plains to California, driven partly by a dogma called "Manifest Destiny" that all North America should share in the ideals of the Republic. In 1846 the "Bear Flag" was raised in California, and later that year the state was annexed to the Union. Wagon train after wagon train creaked across the continent, often having to face hostile Indians, cholera and starvation. Among this great migratory force were the

58

Mormons, who, after violent clashes with non-believers over matters of faith, left Nauvoo, Ill. and headed west under the leadership of Brigham Young to found Salt Lake City in Utah.

The discovery of gold in California in 1848 set in motion yet another milestone in the American heritage. It was the "heritage of the wild west", the good guys versus the bad guys.

Then ho, brothers, ho
To California go;
There's plenty of gold in the world we're told
On the banks of the Sacramento
(Refrain)
The gold is thar, most anywhar,
And they dig it out with an iron bar.

Thus sang the famous troubadour Jesse Hutchinson Jr. in his description of the California Fever which spread throughout the United States, and even beyond its borders, following James W. Marshall's great discovery on the American River near Coloma.

Never before in human history had there been such a call, for here was a chance for the "little man" to get rich. But so often this dream turned to bitter disillusionment, as there just wasn't enough gold for everybody to become a Croesus. Most of the 49ers found that the greatest fortunes were being made in much less exciting occupations than prospecting. Unfortunately for the "poor but honest miner" the stampede attracted many undesirable characters, and at one time there were more mule thieves in business than there were mules. Murder, gambling, intemperance and theft were the evils of the western mining camp. Often, too, public officials were corrupt, and this led honest men to take the law into their own hands by forming Vigilance Committees.

In the wide picture of American development, the California gold rush provided a solid western anchor for the nation's expansion, but linking the eastern seaboard to the west coast through efficient transportation was a problem. The Pony Express was fine for letters and small packages, and Wells, Fargo & Company provided an excellent stage coach and banking system, but these were not sufficient to meet the full needs of the rapidly expanding economy of California. The answer came with the railway. The first such road in the United States, the Baltimore & Ohio, began operation on 14 miles of track on May 24, 1830 using horses to pull the coaches. By 1856 trains were crossing the Mississippi at Rock Island, Ill., but it was not until 1869 that the last spike of a transcontinental railway was driven in at Promontory, Utah.

Meanwhile, on the eastern seaboard away from the "frontier area", telegraph lines were being strung across the land, following Samuel Morse's memorable signal "What hath God wrought", which was carried from Washington to Baltimore on May 24, 1844. In the field of the arts, Harriet Beecher Stowe published "*Uncle Tom's Cabin*" in 1852 and Walt Whitman and Henry W. Longfellow were publishing their most notable works by 1855. Artist, James Whistler became the sensation of Paris in 1862 with his *The White Girl*, and Stephen Foster's ballads, such as *Swanee River* were the hit songs of the day.

Then, in 1861 came four years of civil strife . . ."testing whether that nation, or any nation, so conceived and so dedicated can long endure." (*See pages 68 to 75.*)

After the war, the winning of the West continued, and it was no easy task, as William H. Seward was to find in 1867 when he bought Alaska from the Russians for two cents an acre—a deal almost as fantastic as that of Peter Minuit who bought Manhattan Island for trinkets worth $24 in 1624. General George A. Custer and his 264 men of the Seventh Cavalry found death at the Little Big Horn on June 25, 1876 and Jesse James' gang was riding high, leaving a trail of cold-blooded crimes behind them. These were the days of Wyatt Earp and William Barclay (Bat) Masterson, the frontier marshals, through whose efforts, and others like them, the west was finally won.

But the heritage of the United States does not end here. Like John Brown's soul it "goes marching on". In terms of heritage, the past is but the prologue to the future.

Remember the Alamo!

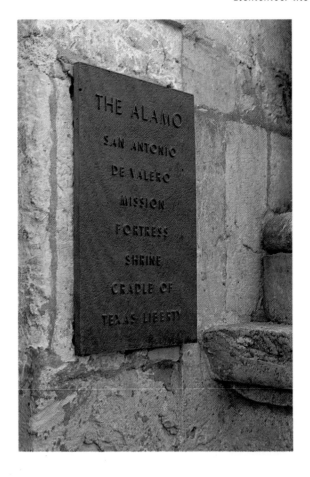

Valley Forge.

ependence Square, Philadelphia, "the most historic square mile in America."

St. John's Church, Richmond, Virginia,
which heard Patrick Henry
make his famous plea,
"Give me liberty or give me death!"

63

The White Dove of the Desert, St. Xavier Del Bac, Tucson, Arizona, one of the most beautiful Spanish missions in the United Stat

An "apartment" dweller at famed Pueblo of Taos, New Mexico.

A young Cherokee brave from the Smoky Mountain area.

While the white man in America was building up *his* heritage the Indian was losing *his*. Amid the cries of "freedom" and "liberty" he found himself driven from his lands and placed on reserves. He was often forced to adopt the white man's language, his ways, his religion and his customs. What is surprising is that any of the Indian heritage survived at all.

Like the white man, he had his great leaders from whom he drew inspiration; men of such caliber as Chief Joseph of the Nez Perce, Sitting Bull of the Sioux, Geronimo of the Apaches, Crazy Horse also of the Sioux, and Hiawatha the legendary chief of the Onondagas who came to life in Longfellow's poem.

In carving, pottery and weaving they showed great artistic skill, but it is a pity they had no writing to preserve all the tales which were told around the campfires.

Today a great effort is being made to preserve and encourage what is left of the Indian culture, for it, too, forms part of the great American heritage.

Evening shadows fall on the desert where once the Indian roamed free.

Long abandoned prehistoric Indian pueblo at Mesa Verde National Park, Colorado.

When the kids go to the old Porter headquarters, now a movie theater in Key West, Florida, they get a double attraction—even if only one film is being shown. For the walls that now ring to the sounds of motion picture entertainment once echoed an entirely different tune.
In 1822 the talk was of pirates and the fact that there were too many of them. Commodore David Porter was ordered to wipe the "Skull and Crossbone" flag from the West Indies. For two years his fleet of 17 ships roamed the seas, netting a total of 79 pirates. With a child's imagination, today the walls of this old building will tell many tales of ships which flew the Jolly Roger from their masts.

Another set of walls which have many tales to "tell" are those of the Spanish fortress, Castillo de San Marcos. Indian workmen cut and fitted the giant blocks of coquina rocks to form the 30 foot high, 12 foot thick walls. Only the tourists have been able to successfully storm its walls.

66

Spanish garden gate, Key West.

Spanish bastion at Castillo de San Marcos,
St. Augustine, Florida. Construction started in 1672.

Robert E. Lee mansion, Arlington, Virginia.

Oak Alley, a typical Southern mansion, built in the 1830s.

The Suwanee, Stephen Foster's "Swanee River."

Drovers Barn, Pioneer Farmstead, Great Smoky Mountains.

The American Civil War, sometimes called the "War between the States", was one of the bloodiest conflicts in the history of man. Once the shooting started there was incredible butchery and brutality, tempered with the occasional show of humanity. Brother fought brother, great cities burned, there were heroes on both sides, and the casualties were staggering in their numbers.

Abraham Lincoln had been president a little more than a month before the first salvoes were fired at Fort Sumter. He was to die from an assassin's bullet six days after General Robert E. Lee surrendered to General Ulysses S. Grant at the Appomattox Court House.

The Confederacy, made up of 11 states, was led by Jefferson Davis, a West Point graduate and former senator from Mississippi who became president on February 22, 1862.

Before the conflict was over, 360,000 Northerners and 258,000 Southerners had died out of the nearly 4,000,000 troops mobilized by both sides.

The North was plunged into debt and the South was ruined.

Gettysburg.

Lincoln's birthplace, near Hodgenville, Kentucky.

coln Memorial, Washington, D.C.

71   *Vicksburg.*

"...We are met on a great battlefield of that war. We have come to dedicate a portion of that field as a final resting-place for those who here gave their lives that that nation might live..."

ABRAHAM LINCOLN   GETTYSBURG, 1863

Stars mark Sherman's hits
on South Carolina
Capitol Building, Columbia.

Lookout Mountain, Chattanooga, Tennes

St. Philip's Church,
Charleston, South Carolina,
built in 1835.
Parish was founded
about 1690.

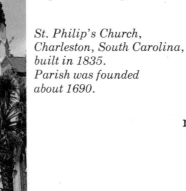

Many great battles were waged and many long
marches were endured before the end came. The
names of men and places are seared into the
American heritage and will never be forgotten.

Cannons are now silent on Vicksburg's hallowed grou

The first White House
of the Confederacy,
Montgomery, Alabama.

The young learn about the past, Chattanod

White House, Washington, D.C.

Jefferson Memorial, Washington, D.C.   *John F. Kennedy's grave, Arlington National Cemetery.*

It is a curious fact that the capital city of the United States is the least American-appearing of all our cities. Washington's stately columnated buildings seemed to have stepped out of some classic age, giving the city an aura of agelessness. In their dignity they stand aloof from the architectural styles of the rest of the city which protects all the heritage and ideals of the nation.

Salt Lake City has a mysticism unlike any other city for its origins were whole-heartedly religious. Temple Square in the heart of the city is the shrine of The Church of Jesus Christ of Latter-Day Saints (Mormon) and this strong, purely American religious denomination speaks out in every facet of life in the Utah capital.

A proud Confederate flag which flies from the dome of the Capitol Building in Montgomery, Alabama, serves as a reminder of the uniqueness of the nation itself.

...erry blossoms and the Washington Monument.

Seagull Monument, Salt Lake City, Utah.

Capitol Building, Washington, D.C.

Temple Square, Salt Lake City.

Thinking big is part of the American heritage, and when it comes to commemorating heroes, words become inadequate. The lands of South Dakota are a case in point. Here in 1927 a sculptor by the name of Gutzon Borglum began to blast out of the side of Mount Rushmore the faces of George Washington, Thomas Jefferson, Theodore Roosevelt and Abraham Lincoln.

The world of sculpture was staggered by the magnitude of the "Shrine to Democracy" project, but was astounded by the one Borglum's associate, Korczak Ziolkowski, undertook on a nearby mountain.

Chief Standing Bear of the Sioux approached Ziolkowski with the suggestion that the Indian heroes should be immortalized, too. The result will be a mountain-size memorial to Chief Crazy Horse, the man who defeated General George Custer at the Battle of the Little Big Horn.

The concept of honoring the Indian moments of greatness will ultimately include a university, hospital and museum complex.

United States Marine Corps war memorial depicting raising of the Stars and Stripes on Iwo Jima, February 23, 1945.

On December 7, 1941, that "day of infamy" at Pearl Harbor, the United States was violently plunged into war to defend with all her might the cherished freedoms gained in 1776. It was not the first time that U.S. servicemen had been called upon to lay down their lives for what they believed. Military cemeteries in Europe attest to the sacrifices of both the First and Second World Wars. In Asia, in Africa, in the Pacific isles and in the United States there are plots of ground which testify to the sacrifices the nation made for freedom.

The USS Arizona memorial at Pearl Har

"Hill of Sacrifice," the National Memorial Cemetery of the Pacific, Punchbowl Crater, Honolulu.

Tomb of the Unknown Revolutionary Soldier, Philadelphia.

*"Ask not what your country can do for you
—ask what you can do for your country."*

John F. Kennedy's Inaugural Address,
January 20, 1961

Our Pastimes

The Declaration of Independence guarantees that all Americans shall be able to follow the "pursuit of Happiness", and if happiness means pastimes then it is the most used section of that great historic document.

Part of the American heritage is to work hard and play hard. The land, the cities and the heritage have all provided Americans with outlets for pleasure and industry strives to provide the tools. So when the factory whistle blows or the clock in the office strikes the hour of closing, the time for recreation begins and, somewhere within the 3,548,974 square miles of land and 66,237 square miles of water which make up this nation, people are going to find it.

To get where he wants to go the American has 41,000 miles of national interstate highways and 3,183,220 miles of rural roads plus other highways and streets on which to travel; 211,384 miles of railway lines; more than 10,000 designated landing fields on which to set his private plane, plus countless miles of trails and pathways.

With all these facilities and an excellent national parks system, national monuments and forests, state parks, city parks and resorts, it is no wonder that Americans take to the open road as often as possible.

But these facilities have not always been available: the man who lifted the United States out of the "pocket knife whittlin', chair rockin' and shade tree settin'" era was a Michigan farm boy by the name of Henry Ford. In 1903, against stiff opposition, he turned out a car called the Model A which cost $800. Subsequently, through mass production, he was able to lower the price of his famed Model T to $290 and by putting America on wheels gave the nation a real shaking up.

Of course, there were people who thought the benzine buggy or horseless carriage would never take the place of the horse and buggy, but today's 97,000,000 cars prove them to have been wrong. The roads of yesterday were appalling by today's standards and when the first transcontinental automobile journey was made in 1903 from San Francisco to New York it took from May 23 to August 1 to complete. This date is almost as important in American history as that of the Lewis and Clark cross-country expedition (they took nearly three *years* to cross in 1803) although historians do not give it the same attention.

There were many advantages to the appearance of the motor car: it made unexpected calls by in-laws and other relatives more frequent; it allowed the government to come up with new means of gathering taxes and it put hundreds of new words, some good and some bad, into our language.

Of greater importance is the fact that it gave the average American the opportunity to see, appreciate and protect the heritage with which his forefathers and nature had endowed him.

Ribbons of black asphalt and white concrete—plus some red tape—tied the country neatly together. Like tribes of itinerant gypsies, the people set out on voyages of exploration. Today mini-cars, old cars, new cars, big cars, station wagons, trailers and campers jam the highways, thruways, turnpikes and lowly roads when the open spaces beckon.

The road and the automobile then have contributed greatly to the American's ability to pursue his favorite pastimes. One of the more relaxing hobbies that the car has brought within easy reach of practically everyone is fishing. The harassed businessman, the tired schoolteacher, the weary salesman all find a common refuge beside a sparkling stream or on the deep waters of a sheltered bay. They leave their daily cares behind the moment they pack the gear, the boxes of tackle, neatly tied flies, hooks, floats, worms, rod and reel and maybe even a frying pan into the trunk of their car and head out for the open road. Peace and tranquility are the rewards for the patient fisherman, together with a finely developed sense of humorous exaggeration if the material rewards weren't quite up to expectation.

In most things American, however, there must be a goal. For many, sitting by an idyllic creek is no way to reach it. In this road game of pastimes the goal might be Old Faithful in Yellowstone Park, the United States' oldest and largest national park, Acadia National Park in Maine, Carlsbad Caverns National Park in New Mexico or Mount Rainier National Park in Washington. Or it might be Grand Canyon, the first of our national playgrounds ever to be seen by a white man. This occurred in 1540 when a Spaniard by the name of Don Garcia Lopez de Cardenas gazed in awe at this great natural wonder.

If the children are travelling too the goal might be that wonderful fantasy of Disneyland which holds a special appeal to children of all ages. Or the interest might lie in following one of the numerous "heritage trails" which criss-cross the New England countryside. There are so many places to go and see in these United States that the mind fairly boggles at the thought of making a selection.

Between "the here" and "the there" are many alluring resorts offering everything from free coffee in the morning to what is practically swimming and skiing at the same time, and, judging by the publicity literature, all are little bits of heaven right here on earth.

Often people in the United States who are looking for a pastime seek out the unusual, and this is as easy as locating a drive-in restaurant or theater. Some like to watch football classic parades where they can admire the gayly decorated floats, ogle the curvaceous baton twirlers who lead the bands or whistle at the beauty queens as they pass by in state. Some even go to the football games and cheer themselves hoarse. World Series baseball games, which are a statistician's dream, draw a much more serious and dedicated crowd because there are neither parades to watch nor baton twirlers or beauty queens to ogle. In this particular pastime it becomes part of a national tradition to remind a certain gentleman, called an umpire, that

his eyesight is impaired and that he suffers from a rather severe form of mental retardation. Hockey, basketball and boxing cards also fill a serious role in the American pastimes, and nobody can doubt the seriousness of professional wrestling.

Participation in preserving the nation's heritage might lead to joining a historical association or, if acquiring and flying World War Two air craft is a passion, this pastime would lead to joining the Confederate Air Force, a fun but serious group with headquarters at Rebel Field, Harlingen, Texas. An interest in California would lead to the Ancient and Honorable Order of E Clampus Vitus, founded in 4005 B.C., a fact which members say can be proved through unwritten documents. There are also lodges and luncheon service clubs to join, for supporting organizations seem to be an integral part of the American pastime heritage.

There is a breed of American who loves to chase railway locomotives and he bands himself together with other addicts to seek out narrow gauge railways, steam engines, incline railways, aerial tramways and even old railway tickets. There are ship-lovers who will grow ecstatic over an old wind-jammer tied up in front of a maritime museum, or an echo of yesteryear in a Mississippi river boat. There are also those who put on scuba gear and explore the ocean depths, perhaps in search of a wrecked Spanish galleon laden with pieces of eight. Admittedly the chances of finding lost treasure at sea or lost mines on land are pretty slim, but in these pastimes, as in all others which Americans follow, the object is to find happiness—a treasure more precious than gold.

American ingenuity has reduced the housewife's burden to a mere bagatelle, allowing her more time for leisure. From these scientific achievements has emerged a unique institution called the "coffee clack". In fairness it should be recorded that men also have their "clacks", although coffee is not necessarily brewed for these occasions. Research has shown that this pastime calls for a deck of cards, a pile of brightly colored chips and a great deal of derring-do. Unlike the more sophisticated game of bridge which is often played in mixed company, the bidding in poker—for that is the name of the game—is often so wild and so complicated it would take a team of Philadelphia lawyers to make any sense out of it.

Another pastime institution is the "cook-out" or "barbecue", a culinary ritual practised in garden patios, on sundecks or apartment balconies and also in the wide open spaces. Here Man is supreme, his status symbol being a chef's hat and apron. The result, hopefully, is a gourmet's delight—on the other hand it could be a disaster.

Almost as nerve-wracking as wondering whether the steak or chicken will burn to a crisp is waiting to see what happens between the commercials on the television screen. This American pastime has greatly encouraged the art of selling soap and human pathos, as well as bringing the world right smack into the living room.

Television—and radio—also bring music into the home, and perhaps music is one of America's greatest pastimes. The nation has not produced a Beethoven or a Brahms but it has produced a style of music which has won world renown as being "American". It has crossed with ease normally tight and restricted international borders and is sung and hummed wherever man expresses his joy with a song. New York's Broadway Musicals, Hollywood films, the popular "big" bands, New Orleans jazz bands, folksingers and the entire recording industry are all geared to satiate the appetite of a demanding public.

The country also hosts some of the finest symphony orchestras and conductors in the world, and a "First Night" of New York's famed Metropolitan Opera is one of the première events of the year.

The movies too are an American pastime which has caught the attention and imagination of the world ever since Thomas Edison gave the first public performance of his Kinetoscope in New York on April 14, 1894. Heroes and heroines of the silver screen are the nation's goodwill ambassadors to the rest of the world.

Exhibitions of painting and sculpture are attracting growing numbers of followers each year and the American reader of both fiction and non-fiction works ranks among the world's best-read citizens.

So when an American says he has nothing to do with his time, *don't you believe him.*

Grand Canyon.

"Howdy, pardner!" is a western greeting for a famous American pastime, the rodeo. Roping and wrestling steers, riding Brahma bulls and bareback riding are all in a day's work for the cowboy.

"Gee, I wish I had more money."

91

Since 1911, the Indianapolis Motor Speedway has been the mecca of racing fans.

America's car racing classic, the 500 at Indianapolis, Indiana.

Greyhound racing at Daytona Beach, Florida.

Detroit Tigers.

Maybe a star is being born here.

Sports, participant or spectator, are the kings of pastimes in the United States. The fanfare is not one of trumpets but of names: baseball, basketball, football, hockey, golf, boating, horse, dog and car racing, for a few examples. In America it is said that everybody has a chance to become President, and in the wide arena of sport it can just as truthfully be said that everybody has a chance to become a star. A major league scout could be watching a sand-lot baseball game and send some boy into the big time; a caddy might turn out to be a golf "pro" and the kid down at the gas station who tinkers with your car could end up at Indianapolis. Even the family dog, if he's a greyhound, could be a runner at Daytona Beach. *Could* and *might?* This is the United States, where anything is possible.

Teeing off near Salt Lake City.

Power boats at Grand Teton National Park.

*Lookout Mountain Incline Railway,
Chattanooga, Tennessee.*

Oh, deer.

94

Hiking near Brigham Canyon, Utah.

"What's the plural of 'moose'?"

"Whatcha got to eat?"

Joshua Tree National Monument.

Carlsbad Caverns, New Mexico.

Niagara Falls, the honeymoon capital of America.

The sounds of a pastime can be as varied as those emanating from a juke box in a discotheque. The most delightful, of course, is that of the squeals of delight from little children as they become aware of the great variety of things to be done and seen in the world about them. Listen to them at the circus, at a zoo, at Disneyland, at a rodeo or at the beach, and laugh along with them.

The sounds that produce squeals of delight from an adult are more sophisticated, but just as contagious as the laughter of youngsters. A jazz combo in New Orleans can bring about a different kind of squeal than say the sound of a person who has just hit the jackpot at a Nevada slot machine.

In the United States laughter is as much a part of the way of life as paying taxes—one of the few facets of life in this country which isn't fun.

Waiting for the jackpot, Reno, Nevada.

Lincoln Center, New York City.

The down beat in New Orleans.

Reno, "the biggest little city in the world" at night.

Pounding surf in Hawaii.

Youthful calypso band at Key West, Florida.

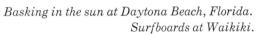

Basking in the sun at Daytona Beach, Florida.
Surfboards at Waikiki.

Imprints of the stars,
Grauman's Chinese Theater, Hollywood.

The call of the pounding surf on a warm stretch of sandy beach is inescapable to most people. If the call is answered, and in America there is no reason why it can't be, good times lie ahead such as riding the crest of a wave on a surf board, soaking up the sun or just plain loafing.

There are other attractions to a sunny clime as well. These include listening to a calypso band at Key West, Florida, or walking in the footsteps of a movie idol in Hollywood, California.

101

*Indian crafts for sale
in Santa Fe, New Mexico.*

Sending a post card home.

Posing for a street art

Ever see a chipmunk that wasn't hungry?

*The man on the flying kite,
Cypress Gardens, Florida.*

No text book is required to tell Americans how to spend their vacations. For some it might call for athletic prowess, such as "kite flying", water skiing and pedal boating, while to others it might provide the opportunity for picking up rumpus room knick-knacks in some quaint curio or antique store.

America the Beautiful, from city-bound Central Park to Yellowstone, from animals in the zoo to those in their natural habitat, offers something for everybody.

And when the trip is over, memories of the beautiful things seen and the exciting things done, will long linger in the mind.

Baby gorilla, San Diego zoo.

Anything for a peanut!

Water ski show at Cypress Gardens.

A peaceful setting in New York's Central Park.

102

Boy meets parrot.

Pedal boating.

San Diego harbor.

Trying to outsmart a trout.

"Blue Angeles" at rest formation . . .

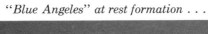

A luau in Hawaii.

Old Faithful, Yellowstone National Park.

. . . and in flight.

103

National Art Gallery, Washington, D.C.

104

Looking Forward

In a few years time the United States of America, born to the sounds of fife and drum and cannon fire, will celebrate its 200th anniversary.

There will be many occasions during these festivities to take a long hard look at the progress this nation has made during these two great and exciting centuries. Two hundred years ago, the United States clung to the eastern seaboard with only 13 states. Today there are 50 of them, stretching from the Atlantic to mid-Pacific and to the polar sea. Though the United States has changed in size the same basic ideals which led Thomas Jefferson to take pen in hand and write the Declaration of Independence still prevail. The message read that fourth day of July 1776 is as real today as it was then. It has been preached, discussed and defended all over the world, sometimes at a terrible cost in human lives and suffering.

The men who affixed their names to this document were, above all, humanists, and it is in terms of humanity that their words ring out today. If those men could return to see the product of their creation they would be surprised, and perhaps a little disturbed. They would see the wonders of a technological age and they would learn that a successor to that flag which came into existence at the Second Continental Congress in Philadelphia on July 14, 1777, is now embedded in the lunar surface, placed there by an American astronaut. They would also see that the world is a great deal more complicated in the 1970s than it was in the 1770s and well might they mark the words of one of their contemporaries, Thomas Paine, who said, "These are times that try men's souls".

As humanists they would remind us that the very background of this nation's greatness lies in its understanding of the human spirit. This message is particularly important when it might seem that certain branches of science, aided and abetted by the computer, are set to take over the world. It is true that the whole course of our lives is being changed by scientists and there are bound to be complaints. Printers once cried out that the end of the world was upon them when the linotype machine was introduced, but there are now more men engaged in that craft than there ever were. Change does not mean doom, but rather it means just the opposite. Just as the leaders of 200 years ago would note a change today, the contemporary leaders would be equally amazed if they could drop in on the world another two centuries in the future.

Though scientific achievements of one day might be outdated by another discovery the following day, there is one thing which never changes and that is the striving for a better way of life for all people. In this goal, the "pure" scientist and the humanist must march hand in hand, giving credit to each other for their dual role in the attainment of this goal. But sometimes this progress moves too fast and by so doing things are put out of perspective and what emerges is a confused picture. Militant groups, small in numbers but loud in voice, cry out that there is a "sickness" upon the land, and they are sometimes so confused by the changes that are taking place that they fail to think about what is really being done to make these United States a better place in which to live.

By keeping in perspective the role the arts and sciences play, many of the causes of today's "sickness" can be corrected. In the immediate years to come this close association will be of utmost importance for the humanities are like a conscience, and if its voice is ignored in the race of acquired technological knowledge the result will be a nation of Orwellian robots. Just as a steel span must have a solid base, so the bridge into the future must have a solid foundation and the rock on which it will be built will always be "understanding the human point of view".

The sciences have many branches and the humanities also have their long list of disciplines, and all are dedicated to one particular goal—the advancement of man's welfare.

The "recording humanity" of the arts is the one the confused and befuddled should look to for help. In the treasure houses of American arts can be found an imperishable record of man's past achievements which can be a solace and an inspiration in these difficult times.

No nation on earth has had better chroniclers than the United States. Few, if any, nations have better facilities for displaying and bringing to the attention of the people the accrued knowledge of the ages to aid them in "Looking Forward". Major cities like New York, Chicago, San Francisco and Washington have world renowned galleries, public and private, which cater to all those who use them. There is scarcely a community of any size which does not have a public library, nor a drug store that does not have a book rack.

Books, wrote the American poet Stephen Vincent Benét, are:

...man's memory and his aspiration
The link between his present and his past,
The tools he builds with.

From the printed page, the photographer's negative and the artist's canvas have come pictures that frame the very essence of our life. New artists and new writers, traditionalists and avant garde, are rising steadily toward the heights attained by their predecessors and with pen and brush are eloquently recording our times through their individual imagery.

The power of the written word has never been felt more strongly than in the Constitution of the United States, with all its sacredly guarded humanitarian principles.

"We, the people of the United States", reads the preamble to the original seven articles, "in order to form a more perfect Union, establish justice, insure domestic tranquility, provide for the common defense, promote the general welfare, and secure the blessings of liberty to ourselves and our posterity..."

Since that day in 1787, when George Washington sent it to Congress, the Constitution has undergone several changes, mostly on humanitarian grounds. Under it slavery was abolished, equal rights for white and colored citizens were established and nation-wide women's suffrage was granted. (Income tax was also established and prohibition was granted and taken away by Constitutional amendments, but whether or not these were humanitarian is still widely debated.)

Under this aura of humanitarianism, forces within "the people of the United States" worked out formulae for their "general welfare" and the once downtrodden working man achieved a dignity by peaceful means which his counterparts in other areas of the world could not achieve even by armed revolt against their oppressors.

Through various government and private agencies, the humanitarian message has been shipped abroad in the form of medical supplies, food and technology for the relief of under-developed nations and for the assistance of those stricken by major catastrophes dealt to them by nature and by the hand of their fellow man.

One of America's greatest inventors, Alexander Graham Bell, the father of the telephone, was a man marked by a great devotion to the well-being of the people. Though honors were heaped upon him for his inventions and his scientific experiments, he always looked upon himself as being just a "teacher of the deaf".

It has happened that scientific achievements which have proved to be a boon to mankind didn't start out with a humanitarian base. But, as in the case of the release of atomic energy, basic human principles came to the fore and nuclear fusion, born in war, was tamed to play a peaceful and meaningful role as a servant of peace. It works the other way too. When the Wright Brothers flew their ungainly creation for 12 seconds on December 17, 1903, they could not possibly have realized how the whole course of transportation—and war—would be changed. In fact man's whole outlook on the world about him took a turn that day and since then it has never looked back. For the space age was born that day at Kitty Hawk, North Carolina.

What lies ahead is exciting and at the same time terrifying. The problems of world population will grow more acute and more demands will be made on man's humanitarian instincts. There will be the troubling questions of food supply, proper usage of the land, employment and transportation. Just as aviation has progressed

First plane to cross the Atlantic, Charles A. Lindbergh's "Spirit of St. Louis" has a place of honor in the Smithsonian Institution, Washington, D.C.

from the first decade of this century until the present, other sciences now in their embryo state will reach their full bloom, and it would take more than a Nostradamus to predict which of those studies now in its infancy will rise to major heights.

Difficult though the times ahead may be, there is no reason to toll the bells of doom, for in the words of John Donne, "No man is an Iland, intire of itselfe; every man is a peece of the Continent, a part of the maine . . . any man's death diminishes me, because I am involved in Mankinde."

One of the most deeply rooted institutions in the United States is the schoolroom and it is here that the first steps to meet the challenge of the future will be made. American educational systems have never shirked their responsibility in this regard and although for them these also are "times that try men's souls" they will not fail now or in the future.

The constantly changing pattern of American life presents to the educator his

107

greatest challenge. Leisure is increasing as manual labor decreases, and the problems of an affluent society are mounting steadily.

Here again, the combination of pure and humanitarian sciences must be welded together before irritating questions get out of hand, for while man may be walking on the lunar surface he has not left a Utopia behind. But just as Dr. Jonas Salk lifted the fear of polio from the world, other men and women will come forward with an answer to the problems which beset us today.

On the memorial to the philanthropist William Ellery Channing in the Public Garden, Boston, are these words taken from his writings:

"I see the marks of God in the heavens and the earth; but how much more in a liberal intellect, in magnanimity, in unconquerable rectitude, in a philanthropy which forgives every wrong, and which never despairs of the cause of Christ and human virtue: I do and I must reverence human nature. I bless it for its kind affections. I honor it for its achievements in science and art, and still more for its examples of heroic and saintly virtue. These are the marks of a divine origin and the pledges of a celestial inheritance; and I thank God that my own lot is bound up with that of the human race."

If everybody could find their lot bound up with that of the human race, the land would be a happier, cleaner and greener place on which to live.

Hall of Explorers, National Geographic Society, Washington, D.C.

Smithsonian Institution, Washington, D.C.

Millions of years ago, gigantic dinosaurs and other monsters lumbered over the land and wallowed in the mud in the sure and certain knowledge that all was well. Unfortunately for the species they were mistaken, for the prehistoric world was changing too fast and these creatures couldn't take the pace. So they left their bones to fossilize in the primeval sediment. Eons passed, until one day they became an exhibit in a museum.

It was a lack of understanding of the land about them that brought about the downfall of these giants, and the land still demands the understanding of the creatures who dwell upon it. The price of ignorance is high, although fossilization may not be a threat anymore.

Ignorance has been the cause of many a blight. It created the ghastly dustbowls of the Mid-west in the 1930s, and left black sores on the land when coal was ripped in wild abandon from the earth of Kentucky with no heed to the future.

Although man's achievements may take him away from the land, even the Earth itself, nonetheless he is still dependent upon the land for everything he needs. If it were not for the minerals in the land there could be no rocket trips into outer space, nor for that matter could there be automobiles, trains or giant luxury ocean liners.

The minerals are in the ground for the taking, but there is a catch to this generosity. Crops that grow in the earth can be replaced annually by new growth, but there is a finality to harvesting the mineral resources of the land, for in no way can they ever be replaced once they have been removed. "Waste not, want not" is an old and powerful maxim and forward-looking people and industries have made a science out of it called "conservation" so that never again will a resourceful land be so horribly treated.

It is unfair and improper to charge the mining industry with sole responsibility in matters which require conservation, for they are leading the crusade to correct the mistakes of the past. All society must share in the blame and pledge itself to practise conservation wherever possible lest we become scarred by the brand of history that only man is vile.

When life emerged from the sea and began the struggle for existence on the land, it was a giant step forward in the evolution of the earth as we know it today. Now another step forward must be taken—a return to the sea.

The oceans are truly the last frontier on the earth and in them may well depend man's survival. The challenge is there, but how he goes about answering the call is more vital than the end result of his activities. In matters concerning water, man has created a "devil's brew" of a problem for himself which is nothing less than a national disgrace. Pollution from many sources has killed Lake Erie and threatens other lakes and streams. What of the sea? The answer is a direct challenge to the future.

On every coast of the United States there is a large and important fishing industry, but basically it is a primitive one which needs heavy doses of scientific knowledge to make it fulfill its destiny as a major food supplier to a world which is undergoing an immense population explosion.

Millions of dollars are now being spent by the United States and other maritime nations on marine research. Experts claim that an acre of sea water can be just as productive as an acre of land, and the oceans cover 70 per cent of the earth's surface. Beneath the rolling waves of the sea grow half of all living things and vast reserves of gold, silver, tin, magnesium, iron and titanium lie below the ooze of the ocean floor.

The exploration of what some scientists call "inner space" will reveal astonishing riches, but the physicists, biologists, geologists, chemists, mathematicians and all others concerned with the science of oceanography have much to learn before this bonanza can be utilized.

In the future the world under the path of ships may not only supply high protein foods, specially "farmed" under ideal conditions, but also building materials, clothes, sites for nuclear power plants and aids for controlling the weather. Perhaps the sea can stave off the disaster of air pollution, for at the rate man is using "fossil fuels" he will add 75 per cent more carbon dioxide to the air by the beginning of the next century than it now contains. Scientists are hoping to find some way to use the oceans to absorb this toxic menace.

The pioneers who go under the sea in strange looking submergence vehicles could well be the advance guard of a stampede of human lemmings rushing to the sea, not to die, but to live.

Man has never taken anything from the earth which has so quickly revolutionized his way of life to the same extent as oil.

When Edwin L. Drake brought in the first well at Titusville, Pennsylvania in 1859 he ushered in the age of the automobile, mass production, mechanized farming and highly complex industries which provide scores of jobs and challenges for the enquiring mind.

On the land and at sea, the petroleum industry prospers, making the United States the world's leading producer. Forests of steel towers form part of the landscape of a dozen of the 50 states of the Union. But the nation's production alone is not sufficient to meet mounting demands and more must be imported. Thousands of miles of pipelines

carry the crude oil to refineries, and still
more thousand of miles of pipe convey
natural gas into the homes of America. In
steel rolling mills across the country, more
miles of drill pipe and casing are being
manufactured to serve an industry that
shows no signs of relaxing.

New discoveries in Alaska reveal trillions
of barrels waiting to be coaxed out of the
ground, and below the bottom of the sea lie
an estimated 150 trillion cubic feet of
natural gas and 2.5 trillion barrels of oil.
A barrel, by the way, consists of 42 gallons
of petroleum.

Just about every facet of our life is geared
to the petroleum industry, and the doors of
research into the future of this "black gold"
have hardly even been opened.

Boeing 747 jet airliner, the largest airplane ever designed for commercial service, a product of the Pacific Northwest.

Every minute of the day aerial caravans streak across the trackless sky. Breakfast on one side of the continent and lunch on the other is a commonplace occurrence as the United States continues to be a "nation in a hurry".

Hoover Dam.

Oregon pulp mills.

Salt evaporation plant, Utah.

Pittsburgh.

The power of a great nation lies in its industrial strength. No nation on earth can hope to beat the production output of the United States which has two non-secret secrets to impart: free enterprise and mass production.

Once it was a common belief that "big industries" thrived on the amount of black smoke they could produce. Not today, however, for industry is becoming more and more aware of its responsibility toward the community, and the words "air pollution" have become its conscience. Billions of dollars are being spent to control this problem, and Pittsburgh, once known as the "Smoky City" is a leader in the field.

Baton Rouge, Louisiana.

Ever since man first raised his eyes toward the heavens, the moon and the stars have been a source of wonderment. He planned his life by them and later he was able to steer his course, far from home, by his knowledge of the skies. The invention of the telescope by the Italian, Galileo, and his discovery that the moon was not a polished sphere, set off a new wave of inquisitiveness. Man dreamed of going there, but will power alone wasn't enough.

After World War II the science of rocketry had developed sufficiently to permit full-scale planning for a voyage into space. On May 5, 1961, Alan Shephard was thrown 116.5 miles into space for a period of 15 minutes. Twenty days later President John F. Kennedy announced the start of a program to put a man on the moon.

In the succeeding years the United States poured 51 billion dollars into the program. Step by step, through the Mercury, the Gemini and finally the Apollo programs, the United States moved closer to its goal. The first successful orbit of Sputnik I hurtled the world into the space age. The question then asked was: "Who would be the first on the moon?"

Human brains went into action alongside electronic brains as the space race swung into high gear. There was excitement in the air on February 20, 1962, as John Glenn's Mercury 6 waited for the count-down. Then . . . Blast Off! And for the first time an American went into orbit. The eyes of the nation were glued to their television sets that day and a sigh of relief went up when his capsule was fished from the sea after circling the earth three times.

Questions man had never asked previously now needed fast answers before the next step was taken, and these answers resulted in more questions. And so the space program progressed. The masses of technical data being assembled staggered the layman and the pilots of the various flights became national heroes.

And when the moment of triumph arrived and man was on the moon, the whole world paused to pay tribute to the ingenuity of this nation which, in the name of "peace for all mankind", had made one of man's most ancient dreams come true.

With the landing on the moon, the teams of experts were faced with new challenges, and preconceived concepts were hastily discarded. The moon is no longer the great frontier it used to be; it will now be harnessed for the good of mankind. A new dimension in space travel lies ahead. The solar system beckons.

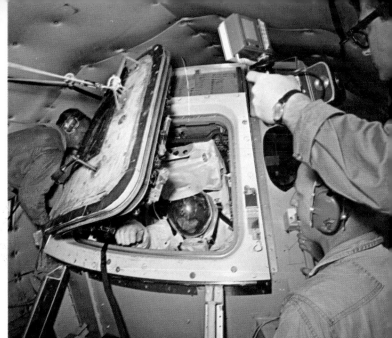

Testing.

Space center, Houston, Texas.

Lift-off Apollo Mission.

Recovery.

For the first time man can see his home planet
from the far reaches of outer space.

Glacier Bay, Alaska.

126

The land can be a stern taskmaster. It can be hard and it can be cruel. Man must always adapt his ways to the land. In return, the land gives sustenance, beauty and opportunity. No matter what man accomplishes, one thing is clear—*under all is the land*.

Produced by Quest Travelbooks Ltd. Vancouver, B.C.
Photography: Ted Czolowski and Toby Rankin
Lithography: The Lakeside Press, R. R. Donnelley & Sons Company

Picture Credits:
United States Air Force Academy   Page 82
Detroit Tigers   Page 93
Boeing Limited, Seattle   Pages 116-117-123
Space program, NASA   Pages 122-124-125